JOHN RIGGS

Play to Learn

Increase Student Outcomes Through Meaningful Play

Contents

Preface

A New Adventure in Learning: The Fun World of Gamification

Welcome, educators! Have you ever thought about making learning as exciting as playing a video game? That's what this book, "Gamification for Beginners," is all about. It's like a guide to turn your classroom into a fun and adventurous place, where lessons feel more like games.

Imagine if students could earn points, get badges, or even top leaderboards, just like in their favorite games, but for doing great in class! This isn't just about making school fun; it's about making learning something students look forward to. And the best part? They learn more and better this way!

In this book, we're going to explore how the magic of games can make education more engaging. We're not just putting game stickers on textbooks. We're talking about changing the way we teach so that every student feels like they're on an exciting learning mission.

Games are awesome because they make us want to keep trying, even when things get tough. They give us little rewards that make us happy and encourage us to do more. What if homework and class projects could make students feel that way too? That's what gamification does. It turns challenges into fun missions and hard work into exciting achievements.

We know that every student is different. Some love reading, some love solving puzzles, and some love being creative. This book will show you how to use gamification to make sure every student finds something in class that they love. This way, everyone can have a good time learning.

But, remember, using games in education is like a special recipe – it needs the right ingredients and balance. This book will be your cookbook. We will share stories of how other teachers have made their classes more game-like and fun. We'll also talk about some common mistakes to avoid.

So, let's get ready to make learning an adventure, where every student is the hero of their own story. Let's make our classrooms places full of excitement, challenges, and joy. Welcome to the world of gamification in education – let the games begin!

$$1$$

Introduction to Gamification in Education

What is Gamification?

Imagine walking into a classroom where learning feels like an adventure, where each student is not just a learner but an active participant in a thrilling quest for knowledge. This is the essence of gamification in education. It's not just about playing games; it's a transformative approach that incorporates game elements into learning experiences, making education engaging and interactive. By introducing elements like points, levels, challenges, and rewards, we turn the traditional learning environment into a dynamic and motivational space. Think of it as a bridge, linking the joy of gaming with the seriousness of education, leading to an immersive learning experience that captivates and educates simultaneously.

The Psychology Behind Gamification

Why does gamification work? It's rooted in fundamental psychological principles. Our brains are wired to enjoy games – they release dopamine, creating a sense of enjoyment and reinforcing the desire to continue playing. Gamification taps into these neurological pathways. For instance, when students earn points for completing tasks, they experience a sense of achievement and progress. Similarly, leaderboards and badges tap into their competitive spirits and need for social recognition. By leveraging these psychological triggers, gamification turns learning into a deeply engaging and emotionally rewarding process.

Historical Perspectives

The story of gamification in education is a fascinating journey through time, reflecting humanity's longstanding desire to make learning engaging and effective. Long before the term 'gamification' was coined, elements akin to it were being used in various forms. In ancient civilizations, learning often involved elements of play and competition, essential for training young minds in skills ranging from strategy to physical prowess. In the Middle Ages, for instance, educational games were employed in the training of knights, blending physical skill development with moral and ethical education. Moving into the Renaissance, educational philosophers like John Locke and Jean-Jacques Rousseau advocated for learning methods that incorporated play and curiosity, recognizing the natural inclination of humans towards game-like challenges.

In the 20th century, the intersection of psychology and education brought a more structured approach to incorporating game elements in learning. B.F. Skinner, an American psychologist, introduced the concept of operant conditioning, which became a foundational principle for game-based learning. Skinner's 'teaching machines', developed in the mid-20th century, were early forerunners of today's gamified learning tools. They used principles of reinforcement to encourage learning, a concept that is central to many modern gamification strategies. The advent of digital technology in the late 20th and early 21st century was a turning point, leading to the proliferation of educational video games and digital learning platforms. These advancements paved the way for the formal recognition and widespread adoption of gamification in educational settings.

The term 'gamification' itself emerged in the digital age, gaining prominence in the early 2000s. It initially found its footing in the business and marketing world, where game elements were used to increase customer engagement and loyalty. Observing its success in these fields, educational theorists and practitioners began to explore its application in learning environments. The introduction of gamified systems in education was met with enthusiasm, as educators saw the potential for these tools to increase student engagement, motivation, and participation. The evolution of gamification in education is a testament to the enduring quest to make learning not just an obligation, but a compelling and enjoyable journey. As we stand in the 21st century, gamification represents the culmination of centuries of educational innovation, blending the old with the new, and setting the stage for a future where learning and play are inextricably linked.

* * *

Core Elements of Gamification

Gamification in education is built upon several key elements, each playing a distinct role in transforming the learning experience. Understanding these core components is essential for effectively integrating gamification into educational contexts.

Points: Points are the quintessential element of gamification. They serve as a quantifiable measure of progress and achievement. In an educational setting, points can be awarded for a variety of actions, such as completing assignments, participating in class discussions, or showing improvement in certain skills. Points not only provide immediate feedback but also help in tracking a student's journey over time, offering a clear representation of their effort and accomplishments.

Badges: Badges act as symbols of achievement and milestones. In the classroom, they can be used to recognize students for mastering specific skills, completing challenging tasks, or demonstrating exceptional behavior. Badges serve as visual and tangible rewards that students can collect and take pride in. They also add an element of collectibility and personalization to the learning experience, as each student can have a unique set of badges reflecting their individual journey.

Leaderboards: Leaderboards introduce a competitive edge to learning. They display rankings based on points or other metrics, fostering a sense of competition among students. However, it's crucial to use leaderboards sensitively in educational environments to ensure they motivate rather than discourage students. A well-designed leaderboard can encourage students to push their boundaries, while also promoting a healthy, collaborative atmosphere where everyone's efforts are recognized.

Challenges and Quests: Challenges and quests transform learning objectives into engaging tasks. These elements can range from simple quizzes to complex projects, designed to test and develop specific skills or knowledge. Challenges should be tailored to the learners' abilities, ensuring they are neither too easy nor too hard. Quests, on the other hand, are longer, more involved tasks that can span several lessons or topics, providing an overarching goal for students to work towards.

Storylines and Narratives: Storylines add context and depth to the gamified learning experience. A compelling narrative can turn a series of educational tasks into an adventure, where each lesson or activity becomes part of a larger story. This storytelling aspect can be particularly effective in engaging students emotionally and intellectually, making the learning process more memorable and meaningful.

Feedback and Progress Tracking: Immediate and continuous feedback is a cornerstone of gamification. It helps students understand where they stand, what they need to improve, and how close they are to achieving their goals. Progress tracking tools, such as progress bars or achievement logs, provide visual representations of a student's journey, offering both motivation and satisfaction in seeing how far they have come.

Incorporating these core elements of gamification into education isn't just about making learning fun; it's about creating a rich, interactive environment where students are motivated to explore, achieve, and grow. By thoughtfully integrating points, badges, leaderboards, challenges, storylines, and feedback mechanisms, educators can craft an educational experience that is not only effective but also deeply engaging and personally rewarding for students.

* * *

Gamification and Modern Education

The integration of gamification into modern education represents a significant shift in teaching and learning paradigms. In a world where traditional educational methods often struggle to engage digital-native learners, gamification emerges as a bridge, connecting educational content with the interactive and immersive experiences that students find in their digital lives. This section delves into how gamification is reshaping modern education, highlighting its impact, applications, and the challenges it addresses.

Enhancing Engagement and Motivation: One of the most notable impacts of gamification is its ability to increase student engagement and motivation. Traditional lecture-based teaching methods can lead to passive learning, but gamification transforms the learning process into an active, participatory experience. By incorporating game elements like points, badges, and leaderboards, educators can create a learning environment that encourages students to take initiative, engage more deeply with the material, and feel a sense of accomplishment in their educational journey.

Personalized Learning Experiences: Gamification allows for greater personalization in education. Each student's learning path can be tailored to their individual needs, interests, and learning pace. For instance, game-based learning environments can adapt to different skill levels, providing more challenging tasks for advanced learners and additional support for those who need it. This personalization ensures that every student finds the learning process relevant and challenging, catering to a diverse range of learning styles and preferences.

Fostering Collaboration and Social Learning: Gamification can also promote collaboration and social interaction among students. Group challenges and team-based leaderboards encourage students to work together, share knowledge, and support each other's learning. This collaborative aspect of gamification mirrors the teamwork and social skills that are increasingly valued in today's workforce, preparing students for the collaborative nature of modern work environments.

Developing 21st-Century Skills: Beyond subject-specific knowledge, gamification helps in developing essential 21st-century skills such as critical thinking, problem-solving, creativity, and digital literacy. Gamified activities often require students to think critically, make strategic decisions, and solve complex problems, skills that are crucial in today's rapidly changing world.

Challenges and Considerations: While gamification offers numerous benefits, it also presents challenges that educators must navigate. The design and implementation of gamified learning experiences require careful planning to ensure they are effective and aligned with educational goals. There is also the risk of overemphasis on extrinsic rewards like points and badges, which could potentially overshadow intrinsic motivation for learning. Educators must strike a balance, ensuring that gamification enhances, rather than detracts from, the educational experience.

The Future of Gamification in Education: As we look to the future, the role of gamification in education is likely to grow even more significant. With advances in technology, such as virtual reality and artificial intelligence, the possibilities for creating immersive and personalized gamified learning experiences are expanding. However, the core objective remains the same: to create an educational environment where learning is not only effective but also a joyous and rewarding journey for every student.

In summary, gamification in modern education is much more than a trend; it's a reflection of a broader shift towards more interactive, personalized, and engaging learning experiences. By harnessing the power of game elements, educators are not just teaching content; they are nurturing a generation of learners who are motivated, engaged, and equipped with the skills they need for the future.

Setting the Stage: Preparing for Gamification in Your Classroom

Understanding Your Educational Goals

When you start using gamification in your classroom, the first step is to think about your goals. What do you hope to achieve by adding game elements to your lessons? This part is like planning a trip: you need to know where you want to go before you start.

- **Making Clear Goals:** Ask yourself, "What do I want my students to learn or get better at through these games?" Your goals should be clear and possible to reach. For example, instead of just saying "get better at math," a specific goal could be "help students improve their algebra skills by 20% before the school year ends."
- **Matching Goals with What You Need to Teach:** Your gaming goals should fit with what you are supposed to teach in your class. This means that while your students are having fun with the games, they are also learning what they need to learn.
- **How Games Help Learning:** Think about how games can make learning better. Games can make students feel good when they do something right

and want to keep learning. Some games can make students excited to compete in a fun way, while others can help them learn to work well in groups.

- **Making Games Work for Everyone:** Remember that all your students are different. Some might like to work alone, and others might like to work in teams. Your games should have something for everyone, so all students can enjoy and learn from them.
- **Thinking About the Future:** Don't just think about what you want your students to learn right now. Think about how these games can help them grow and be ready for the future. For example, you can add challenges in the games that need students to try many times before they succeed. This can teach them to keep trying and not give up, even when things are tough.

In short, knowing your goals for using gamification in class means planning carefully. You want to pick games that help your students learn what they need to learn and grow. By doing this, you make learning fun and useful, and you help your students get ready for the future.

Knowing Your Students

Every class is a unique tapestry of personalities, learning styles, and backgrounds. Understanding your students is crucial for effective gamification. What motivates them? What are their interests and challenges? This knowledge will help you tailor the gamified elements to resonate with your students. Remember, the aim is to make learning an experience that every student finds relatable and rewarding. This requires empathy and a deep commitment to understanding the diverse tapestry of learners in your classroom.

Integrating Gamification into Existing Curricula

Now, let's talk about how to fit gamification into the things you're already teaching in your class. It's like adding exciting toppings to your favorite pizza without changing the pizza itself. Here's how to do it:

- **Finding the Right Spots:** Look at your lessons and see where gamification can make them more interesting. Think about which parts of your teaching can become even more fun with games.
- **Making Learning Fun:** The goal is to make learning enjoyable, not just a game. So, choose games or activities that help students learn better and deeper.
- **Using Technology (or Not):** Some games need computers or tablets, while others can be done with paper and pencils. Think about what's possible in your classroom and choose games that fit.
- **Staying True to Learning:** Remember, games are there to help students learn, so don't let them take over the whole lesson. Make sure that the games match what you want to teach.
- **Starting Slow:** You don't need to change everything at once. Start with one or two games and see how they work. Then, you can add more if you and your students like them.
- **Getting Feedback:** Ask your students what they think about the games. Do they like them? Are they helping them learn? Their feedback can help you make the games even better.
- **Being Flexible:** Sometimes, things might not go as planned. That's okay! Be ready to change things if needed. You're the captain of the ship, and you can adjust the course when necessary.

So, integrating gamification into your teaching is like adding fun toppings to your pizza. It's about making learning exciting and enjoyable, all while staying true to what you're supposed to teach. Start slowly, get feedback from your students, and be ready to make changes as needed. It's all about making learning an adventure that your students will love!

Necessary Resources and Tools

Now, let's talk about the things you'll need to make gamification in your classroom a success. Think of these as the tools in your toolbox, just like a handy builder needs the right tools to create something amazing.

- **Digital or Non-Digital:** First, decide if you want to use games on computers or tablets (digital) or games that don't need technology (non-digital). Both can be lots of fun, but it depends on what's available to you.
- **Game Platforms:** If you're going digital, you'll need to choose the right game platforms or apps. Some games are designed for education and can help students learn while having fun.
- **Board Games and Materials:** For non-digital games, you might need board games, cards, or other materials. These can be a great way to make learning more enjoyable.
- **Accessories:** Sometimes, you might need extra things like dice, timers, or tokens to play the games. These add a fun twist to the games.
- **Computer Access:** If you're using digital games, make sure your students have access to computers or tablets. Check that everything works smoothly before starting.
- **Safety and Privacy:** It's important to think about safety and privacy, especially when using technology. Make sure the games you choose are safe for your students and follow any rules or guidelines set by your school or district.
- **Training and Support:** Don't forget about yourself! Make sure you understand how the games work and how to use them in your teaching. Sometimes, game creators offer training or support to help you get started.
- **Budget and Costs:** Some games and materials might cost money, so it's important to plan your budget. See if your school can help with funding or look for free options if needed.

Remember, just like a builder needs the right tools to build a strong house, you need the right resources and tools to create a fun and engaging learning environment in your classroom. Whether you choose digital or non-digital games, safety and training are important, and budget planning is a must. These tools will help you turn your classroom into a place where learning is not just useful but also loads of fun!

Planning and Timing for Gamification Implementation

Now, let's dive into how to plan and decide when to start using gamification in your classroom. It's a bit like preparing for a special event or a big game. Here's what you need to do:

- **Setting a Schedule:** Think about when you want to start using gamification. It could be at the beginning of the school year or at a specific time in your lessons.
- **Choosing the Right Games:** Decide which games or activities you want to use. Remember, you don't have to use them all at once. Start with a few that match your goals.
- **Introducing Games Gradually:** You can introduce gamification bit by bit. Start with one game and see how your students like it. Then, add more games as you go along.
- **Planning Game Sessions:** Think about how long each game session will be. Some games can be short and others longer. It's up to you to decide what fits best.
- **Tracking Progress:** Make a plan for how you'll keep track of your students' progress in the games. This helps you see how well they are doing and if they're learning.
- **Getting Student Feedback:** Ask your students what they think about the games and the timing. Do they enjoy the games? Do they think it's a good time to play them? Their opinions matter.
- **Flexibility Is Key:** Sometimes, you might need to change your plans. That's okay! Be ready to adjust the timing or the games if something doesn't work as expected.
- **Enjoy the Learning Journey:** Most importantly, remember that gami-

fication is about making learning fun. So, enjoy the journey with your students and have fun along the way.

Planning and timing for gamification is like planning for a special party. You decide when to start, which games to play, and how long each game will be. You listen to your students' feedback and make changes when needed. The most important thing is to have fun while learning together!

* * *

In this chapter, we've laid the groundwork for introducing gamification into your classroom. From understanding your educational goals and knowing your students to integrating gamification into the curriculum, selecting the right tools, and planning its implementation – each step is crucial in setting the stage for a successful gamification experience. This preparation is not just about logistics; it's about setting up a framework that allows for an educational transformation, where learning becomes a journey that students embark on with enthusiasm and purpose. As you move forward, remember that the heart of gamification is not just in its tools and techniques, but in its ability to make learning an adventure that captivates and inspires.

3

Designing Gamified Learning Experiences

Identifying Desired Learning Outcomes

Imagine you're setting off on a treasure hunt, and the treasure you seek is knowledge and skills for your students. But before you start, you need to know exactly what treasure you're looking for. In the world of gamified learning, these treasures are called "learning outcomes."

Starting with a Clear Goal: Learning outcomes are like the map that guides your journey. They are the specific things you want your students to learn by the end of a lesson or a set of lessons. For example, you might want them to understand a historical event, solve math problems, or write a persuasive essay.

Measuring Progress: It's important that these learning outcomes are clear and easy to measure. That way, you can track how well your students are doing and if they've reached their destination. Think of it like checkpoints on your treasure map.

Matching Outcomes to Your Goals: These outcomes should match your goals as a teacher. You choose what your students need to learn, and then you create the games and challenges that help them reach those goals.

Keeping It Aligned: It's also essential that these learning outcomes match what your school or district expects students to learn. This way, your treasure hunt aligns with the bigger picture of education.

So, before you dive into the world of gamification, take a moment to identify these desired learning outcomes. Think of them as the treasures you want your students to find on their educational journey. Once you know what you're looking for, you can start designing games and challenges that lead your students to these valuable treasures of knowledge and skills.

Choosing the Right Game Mechanics

Imagine you're building a playground, and each game mechanic is like a different piece of equipment that makes the playground exciting. In gamified learning, these "game mechanics" are the tools that make the learning experience engaging and fun.

Matching Mechanics to Goals: To choose the right game mechanics, you need to think about your learning goals. Each game mechanic serves a specific purpose. For example, if you want to encourage teamwork, you might choose a mechanic that involves cooperation and competition among students.

Balancing Challenge: Games should be challenging, but not too hard. It's like finding the right balance when riding a bike. You want your students to be engaged, not frustrated. So, pick mechanics that fit the level of challenge you want.

Rewarding Progress: Game mechanics can also help you reward your students for their efforts. Points, badges, and other rewards can motivate students to keep playing and learning. It's like earning stickers for doing well in class.

Feedback and Improvement: Think about how the game mechanics provide feedback to students. Feedback helps them understand what they're doing right and where they can improve. It's like having a coach who tells you how to get better at a sport.

Choosing the right game mechanics is a bit like selecting the right ingredients for a recipe. You want to make sure each one enhances the flavor of your gamified learning experience. By matching mechanics to your goals, balancing challenge, rewarding progress, and providing helpful feedback, you create a learning adventure that's not only fun but also effective.

Building a Narrative for Learning

Imagine you're writing a thrilling story, but instead of just reading it, your students get to be the heroes of the tale. That's what building a narrative for learning is all about—creating an exciting storyline that makes learning an adventure.

Educational Storyline: When you build a narrative for learning, you weave the learning content into a storyline. It's like turning your lessons into chapters of a book. For instance, if you're teaching history, the narrative could be an exciting journey through different historical eras.

Characters and Roles: In this educational adventure, your students become the main characters. They take on roles that fit the narrative. They could be explorers, scientists, detectives, or even fictional characters, depending on the subject you're teaching.

Progressive Challenges: Just like in a story, where each chapter builds upon the last, the challenges in your gamified lessons should also progress. Each challenge should lead to the next, creating a sense of adventure and discovery.

Engaging Plot: The storyline should be engaging and capture students' imaginations. It's like a great book that you can't put down because you're eager to see what happens next.

Creating a narrative for learning is like crafting a captivating tale, but with a twist—it's an educational adventure where your students are the heroes. This narrative makes learning not only informative but also exciting and memorable. So, get ready to embark on this educational journey where every lesson is a new chapter in a thrilling story!

Balancing Challenge and Skill

Imagine you're playing a video game. It's fun because it's not too easy, but also not so hard that you want to give up. In gamified learning, finding the right balance between challenge and skill is just as important.

Zone of Proximal Development: Balancing challenge and skill is a bit like finding the sweet spot—what experts call the "zone of proximal development." This zone is where the challenge is just a bit beyond what you already know and can do. It's like climbing a ladder—one rung at a time.

Starting with Simplicity: When you introduce a new game or activity, start with something simple. It's like learning to ride a bike with training wheels. This helps your students get comfortable and build confidence.

Gradual Complexity: As your students get better, you can gradually increase the complexity of the challenges. Think of it like taking off the training wheels and riding on two wheels. It might be a bit wobbly at first, but it gets easier with practice.

Adjusting as Needed: Be flexible. If you notice that a challenge is too easy or too hard for your students, don't hesitate to make adjustments. It's like being a coach who changes the game plan based on how the team is doing.

Balancing challenge and skill is like tuning a musical instrument—you want it to sound just right. When you get it right, your students are engaged, excited, and eager to learn. It's all about making the learning experience enjoyable, not too easy, and not too hard. So, as you design gamified lessons, keep that sweet spot in mind, and watch your students thrive in their educational journey.

Iterative Design and Testing

Imagine you're an inventor creating a fantastic new machine. You wouldn't expect it to work perfectly on the first try, would you? That's where iterative design and testing come in. It's like fine-tuning your invention until it works flawlessly.

Prototyping and Testing: In the world of gamified learning, this process starts with creating a prototype of your gamified lesson or activity. A prototype is like a rough draft—a first version that you use to test your ideas. You then try it out with a small group of students. It's a bit like having a dress rehearsal before the big show.

Gathering Feedback: During testing, you collect feedback from your students. You ask them questions like, "Did you enjoy the game?" and "Did you feel like you were learning?" Their answers are like clues that help you improve your game.

Continuous Refinement: With feedback in hand, you go back to the drawing board and make improvements. It's like an artist adding more details to a painting to make it even more beautiful.

Adapting to Student Needs: Every group of students is unique, and what works for one may not work for another. So, be ready to adapt your gamified lesson based on your students' needs. It's like customizing a bike for each rider.

Iterative design and testing are like taking small steps to make something great. Each test and adjustment bring you closer to creating a gamified learning experience that's engaging, effective, and tailored to your students' needs. So, don't be afraid to refine and perfect your educational adventure— just like an inventor making a groundbreaking invention.

4

Engagement and Motivation through Gamification

Types of Player Motivations

Imagine you're playing a game. Why do you want to keep playing? What makes it fun and exciting? In this part of our book, we're going to talk about why students, like you, might find learning more interesting when it's like playing a game.

First, let's think about what motivates us. Motivation is the feeling that makes us want to do something. When we play games in class, there are three big reasons that can make us want to learn more. These are like secret ingredients that make the game tasty for our brain!

1. **Choosing What to Do (Autonomy)**: This means you get to make your own choices. Just like choosing your character in a video game, in a gamified class, you might get to choose what kind of questions you want to answer or what activities you want to do. This is exciting because you feel like you're the boss of your own learning.

2. **Feeling Good at Something (Competence)**: This is when you feel like you're getting better at something. In games, you might feel proud when

you reach a new level or beat a tough challenge. In a gamified class, you might feel this way when you understand a new topic or do well on a quiz. It's like leveling up your brain!

3. **Playing with Friends (Relatedness)**: Games are more fun with friends, right? When we play learning games in class, we can work with other students, share ideas, and help each other. It's fun to feel like part of a team and to feel connected with your classmates.

So, when teachers turn learning into a game, they're really trying to tap into these feelings. They want to make you feel excited about making choices, proud of what you're learning, and happy to be working with your friends. These feelings are the secret to making learning feel less like work and more like play. In the next sections, we'll explore how teachers can use rewards, feedback, and teamwork to make learning as fun as your favorite game!

Reward Systems in Educational Gamification

In this part, we're going to talk about rewards in games and how they make learning more fun. Have you ever gotten a gold star for good work or a high score in a video game? That's a kind of reward. In a classroom that uses gamification, rewards are used to make learning exciting and to celebrate your hard work and achievements.

First, let's understand what a reward is. A reward is something you get for doing well or for trying hard. It makes you feel good and encourages you to keep going. In a classroom game, rewards can be many different things. Some rewards might be points you earn for answering questions correctly. Others could be badges you get for finishing a project or a special title like "Math Wizard" for doing really well in math.

These rewards do two important things:

1. **They Make Learning Fun**: Just like how you feel happy when you unlock a new level in a game, getting a reward in class can make you feel excited and happy. It's like the game is cheering for you!

2. **They Help You See Your Progress**: Rewards are like little signs that show you how much you've learned and grown. When you look at the points or badges you've earned, you can see how much you've accomplished. It's like having a map that shows you how far you've traveled in your learning journey.

But remember, the best rewards in gamified learning are not just about getting points or prizes. They're about feeling proud of yourself, enjoying learning, and wanting to learn more. The real reward is becoming smarter and more skilled, and having fun while you do it.

So, when teachers use reward systems in the classroom, they're not just giving out points or stickers. They're helping you see how awesome you are at learning and making the whole experience feel like a fun adventure. Let's keep this adventure going as we explore how feedback and progress tracking in games can help us learn even better!

Feedback Loops and Progress Tracking

Now, let's chat about something really cool in games and learning: feedback loops and progress tracking. Have you ever played a video game where you get points or move to a new level after doing something right? That's a kind of feedback. It tells you, "Hey, you're doing great!" In a classroom, feedback loops and tracking your progress help you know how you're doing in your learning adventure.

Feedback loops in learning are like having a helpful coach. Imagine you're playing basketball, and your coach tells you, "Great shot!" when you score a basket. In the classroom, feedback can be a teacher saying, "Good job!" when you answer a question correctly or giving you tips on how to do better next time. This feedback is super important because it helps you understand what you're doing well and what you need to work on. It's like a guide that helps you on your learning path.

Now, let's talk about progress tracking. Progress tracking is like a treasure map of your learning journey. It shows you where you started, how far you've come, and where you're headed next. In a gamified classroom, this might look like a chart on the wall that tracks your points, or maybe a special booklet where you collect stickers for each new thing you learn. This is really cool because it lets you see all the progress you've made. It's like looking at a photo album and seeing how much you've grown.

Here's why feedback loops and progress tracking are so important:

- **They Keep You Motivated**: Just like how a scoreboard in a game keeps you excited and wanting to score more points, seeing your progress in class keeps you motivated. It's exciting to see yourself moving forward and getting better.
- **They Help You Learn Better**: With good feedback, you understand what you're good at and what you need to practice more. It's like having a personal learning map that shows you the best way to go.

So, in a classroom with gamification, feedback loops and progress tracking are like having a cheering squad and a map. They cheer you on and show you the way, making learning not just more fun but also more effective. Up next, we'll explore how working and playing with friends can make learning even more awesome!

Encouraging Peer-to-Peer Interaction

In this part, we're going to dive into a super fun aspect of gamified learning: playing and learning with your classmates, which we call peer-to-peer interaction. It's like having your friends as teammates in a game. When you learn with others, it's not just more fun, but you also learn better!

Think about your favorite multiplayer game. What makes it so much fun? Probably playing with others, right? In the classroom, when learning becomes like a game, you get to work with your classmates in a similar way. This could mean teaming up to solve a puzzle, competing in a friendly quiz, or helping each other to understand a new topic.

Working with your friends in class has some awesome benefits:

- **You Learn From Each Other**: Sometimes, your friends can explain something in a way that just makes more sense. Or maybe you're the one who's really good at something and can help your friends understand. It's like each of you has your own superpower, and together, you make a super team!
- **It Makes Learning More Exciting**: Just like how a game becomes more thrilling when you play with others, learning with your friends makes the classroom feel like an adventure. It's fun to share ideas, challenge each other, and celebrate together when you solve a problem or win a game.
- **You Feel More Connected**: When you work and learn together, you feel like you're part of a team. This makes school feel like a friendly and fun place, where everyone is working together towards the same goal. It's like being part of a club where everyone supports each other.

So, in a gamified classroom, your teacher will create activities that let you and your classmates work together. This is not just to make learning fun, but also to help you build friendships, learn from each other, and feel like you're part of a special learning team. Next, we'll look into how gamification can be great for all kinds of learners, making sure everyone has their own way to shine!

Gamification for Diverse Learning Styles

Let's talk about how gamification in the classroom is awesome for all kinds of learners. Everyone learns in their own special way. Some of us like to read and write, some of us love to do things with our hands, and some of us learn best when we listen or watch. Gamification is like a magic box that has something for everyone, no matter how you like to learn!

When learning becomes a game, it's not just about reading from books or listening to the teacher. It can involve all sorts of activities that match different learning styles. Let's explore how:

- **For Those Who Love Stories and Imagination**: Do you like reading stories or making up your own? In a gamified classroom, you might go on a learning adventure where you're the hero of a story. You'll solve problems, complete quests, and maybe even create your own story as part of the learning process.

- **For the Hands-On Learners**: If you love building, drawing, or moving around, gamification has got you covered too. You might find yourself building a model, drawing a poster, or even acting out a scene to learn a new concept. It's like learning by doing, and it makes understanding new things so much more fun.
- **For the Thinkers and Problem Solvers**: Some of us love puzzles and challenges. Gamified learning can turn lessons into exciting challenges where you need to think critically, solve puzzles, or answer tricky questions to progress in the game.
- **For Those Who Learn by Listening and Watching**: And if you love listening to stories or watching things, there are games that include videos, music, and spoken instructions. You might watch a fun video or listen to a story that teaches you something new.

The cool thing about gamification is that it lets everyone find their own way to learn. Whether you like to create, solve, play, or imagine, there's always a way to make learning fit just right for you. It's like having a learning adventure that's tailor-made, just for you!

So, through gamification, teachers can make sure that every student gets to learn in the way that suits them best. This way, everyone gets a chance to shine in their own unique way. Now, aren't you excited to see how fun and special learning can be with gamification? Let's keep exploring and find out even more!

5

Technology and Tools for Gamification

In the dynamic landscape of modern education, the integration of technology has become a cornerstone of innovative teaching methods. Gamification in education is no exception. This chapter delves into the diverse array of tools and technologies available to educators, guiding you through the selection and implementation of the most effective resources to gamify your classroom.

Digital Platforms and Apps

As educators in the K-12 system, it's essential to stay abreast of the digital tools that can revolutionize the way we teach. Digital platforms and apps are not just about bringing new technology into the classroom; they're about enriching the learning experience in ways that resonate with today's tech-savvy students.

When we talk about digital platforms and apps, we're referring to a wide range of educational software. These can be apps that gamify math or language learning, websites that offer interactive science experiments, or platforms that allow students to embark on virtual field trips. The key is to find digital tools that are not only engaging but also align with educational goals and curriculum standards.

For instance, imagine a math app that turns algebra into a quest to unlock ancient mysteries. Each problem solved brings the student closer to the treasure. This kind of interactive learning not only makes math more appealing but also helps students develop problem-solving skills.

Another important aspect of digital platforms is their ability to personalize learning. Many apps come with adaptive learning technologies that adjust the difficulty level based on the student's performance. This means that students who grasp concepts quickly can be challenged more, while those who need more time can learn at their own pace.

It's also crucial to consider the user experience of these apps. They should have an intuitive interface, making it easy for both teachers and students to navigate. Also, consider the feedback mechanisms. Good educational apps provide immediate feedback, which is crucial for learning. This instant response can motivate students and help them understand concepts better.

In addition to individual learning, many digital platforms facilitate collaborative projects. They can connect students from different classrooms or even different schools, fostering a sense of global community and teamwork.

However, the effectiveness of these tools depends largely on how they are integrated into your teaching. It's not just about using the latest app; it's about how these digital tools complement and enhance your existing teaching methods. This could mean using an app as a supplementary tool for homework or as a central element of a lesson plan.

Non-Digital Tools and Methods

In the midst of our digital age, it's vital for K-12 educators to remember the enduring value of non-digital tools and methods in the classroom. These traditional approaches to learning, from board games to creative storytelling, offer a necessary balance to the tech-heavy aspects of modern education. They encourage social interaction, critical thinking, and the development of skills that are not always fostered by digital means.

Board games, for instance, are a timeless educational tool. They can be seamlessly integrated into various subjects to enhance learning. For example, a history-themed board game can transport students back in time, allowing them to experience historical events or the lives of significant figures in a tangible, interactive way. These games not only make learning fun but also promote strategic thinking and collaboration among students.

Role-playing activities are another powerful non-digital method. They enable students to immerse themselves in different roles, from scientists to literary characters, fostering empathy and a deeper understanding of the subject matter. In a science class, students could role-play as different elements in the periodic table, explaining their properties and how they interact with other elements. This kind of active learning makes abstract concepts more concrete and memorable.

Furthermore, simple tools like flashcards and puzzles serve as excellent resources for reinforcing concepts and enhancing memory skills. Flashcards can be particularly effective for subjects that require memorization, such as vocabulary or scientific terms. Puzzles, on the other hand, are great for problem-solving and can be used in subjects ranging from math to geography.

Art and craft activities also hold significant educational value. They provide a hands-on learning experience and allow for creative expression. For instance, students can create models of the solar system in a science class or dioramas to depict scenes from a novel in a literature class. These activities not only reinforce learning but also help in developing fine motor skills and artistic sensibilities.

It's important to note that while these non-digital methods are effective, their success largely depends on how they are implemented. Educators need to ensure that these activities are well-integrated into the curriculum and aligned with learning objectives. The goal is to create a balanced and holistic educational experience that leverages the strengths of both digital and non-digital methodologies.

Blended Learning Environments

Think of a blended learning environment as a creative classroom recipe, mixing the best parts of technology with traditional learning methods. It's like using different teaching ingredients to create the most engaging and effective learning experience for your students.

In a blended classroom, technology plays a key role. You might use educational apps and websites to introduce new concepts or reinforce lessons. These digital tools are fantastic for individual learning; they offer interactive experiences and instant feedback, which is vital for understanding challenging subjects. For instance, a student struggling with fractions can use an app that visually breaks down the concept, making it easier to grasp.

However, it's not all about screens. Blended learning also means bringing in hands-on, non-digital activities. This could involve group projects, role-playing, or even traditional board games modified for educational purposes. These activities encourage collaboration, critical thinking, and communication skills. For example, while learning about ecosystems, students could work together to build a model rainforest, discussing each layer and the animals that live there.

The real magic of blended learning lies in how these elements are combined. It allows you to tailor your teaching methods to suit different learning styles and needs. Some students may benefit more from interactive digital tasks, while others thrive in group discussions or hands-on activities. By varying your approach, you can ensure that each student finds a way to connect with the material.

Moreover, this approach keeps learning fresh and exciting. One day, students might be on a virtual field trip using tablets, and the next, they're creating posters or conducting experiments in small groups. This variety not only maintains engagement but also helps to develop a wider range of skills.

Blended learning also gives you, as an educator, the flexibility to adapt to various scenarios. Whether it's catering to different learning paces within a single classroom or transitioning between in-person and remote learning, a blended approach provides a robust framework to support your teaching.

Accessibility and Inclusivity in Tech-based Solutions

As K-12 educators, it's crucial to ensure that every student has equal access to learning, especially when integrating technology into the classroom. Accessibility and inclusivity in tech-based solutions are about making sure that every student, regardless of their abilities or backgrounds, can benefit from these tools.

Firstly, accessibility in digital tools means that students with disabilities can use them just as effectively as their peers. This includes students who might have visual or hearing impairments, learning disabilities, or physical challenges. For instance, an educational app should have features like text-to-speech for students who have difficulty reading, or subtitles for those with hearing impairments. Also, the app interface should be easy to navigate for students who might have motor skill difficulties.

Inclusivity, on the other hand, goes beyond just accessibility. It's about creating a learning environment where every student feels represented and valued. This means choosing tech tools that include diverse cultures, languages, and perspectives. For example, a history app should not only focus on Western perspectives but also include stories and histories from around the world.

When selecting digital tools, it's important to consider the varying socio-economic backgrounds of students. Not all students may have access to high-speed internet or the latest devices at home. Therefore, it's essential to choose apps or platforms that work well on a variety of devices, including smartphones, and don't require a constant high-speed internet connection.

Moreover, educators should be trained in using these technologies. Understanding how to adjust settings for accessibility and how to guide students in using these tools is key. Training should also include awareness of cultural sensitivities and diverse learning needs to ensure that teachers can provide the necessary support to all students.

Evaluating and Choosing the Right Technology

Choosing the right technology for your classroom is like picking the perfect tool for a job. It's all about finding what works best for your teaching style and your students' learning needs. With so many options out there, it can be a bit overwhelming, but there are some key things to keep in mind that can help make this decision easier.

First, think about your educational goals. What do you want your students to learn or achieve with this technology? If you're teaching math, maybe you need an app that focuses on problem-solving skills. For a science class, perhaps a virtual lab would be beneficial. The technology you choose should align with what you want your students to learn.

Next, consider the usability of the technology. It should be easy for both you and your students to use. If a tool is too complicated, it can become frustrating and might even take away from the learning experience. Look for technology with a simple, intuitive interface that doesn't require a lot of time to understand.

It's also important to think about compatibility with existing resources. The technology should work well with the devices and software you already have in your classroom. This makes it easier to integrate the new tool into your lessons without having to worry about technical issues.

Another crucial factor is student engagement. The technology should be engaging and interesting to your students. It should grab their attention and make them excited about learning. Whether it's through interactive elements, gamification, or visually appealing content, the tool should motivate students to participate and learn.

Cost is also a key consideration. You'll need to find technology that fits within your school's budget. There are many cost-effective options available, including free and open-source tools. However, it's important to weigh the cost against the quality and effectiveness of the technology.

Finally, don't forget about support and training. The technology should come with good customer support in case you run into issues. Also, consider whether you or your colleagues will need training to use the technology effectively. Some companies offer training sessions and materials, which can be very helpful.

6

Case Studies: Gamification in Action

Elementary School Examples

Let's explore inspiring real-world examples of how gamification has been applied in elementary school classrooms, creating exciting and engaging learning experiences for young students. These stories showcase how gamification strategies have transformed traditional education into interactive adventures that cater to the unique needs of elementary school children, making learning fun and meaningful.

One remarkable example comes from a second-grade classroom where a teacher incorporated a gamified spelling program. Instead of the usual spelling quizzes, the teacher designed a spelling bee game where students took on the roles of spelling champions. The students were divided into teams and had to spell words correctly to advance in the game. They earned points for each correct answer and even had a virtual "spelling trophy" that was awarded to the winning team at the end of each week. This approach not only made spelling lessons exciting but also encouraged healthy competition and teamwork among the students.

Another fantastic instance involves a third-grade math class where math problems were turned into an adventure quest. Students became "math explorers" and had to solve math puzzles to progress in their quest to find hidden treasures. Each correct answer brought them closer to their goal, and they encountered challenges that required them to apply their math skills creatively. This gamified approach not only improved math comprehension but also fostered a growth mindset, as students embraced challenges with enthusiasm.

In yet another case, a kindergarten teacher introduced a gamified reading program that turned reading practice into an interactive journey. Students embarked on a "reading adventure" where they explored different story worlds by reading books. They earned "reading badges" for completing books and reached milestones like becoming "book explorers" or "storybook heroes." This approach not only instilled a love for reading but also celebrated each student's progress, creating a positive reading culture in the classroom.

These elementary school examples demonstrate the power of gamification in capturing the attention and motivation of young learners. By infusing elements of play, competition, and exploration into the curriculum, educators can make learning an exciting adventure for their elementary school students. These gamified approaches not only enhance subject comprehension but also nurture essential skills such as teamwork, problem-solving, and a love for learning.

* * *

Middle School Case Studies

Next, we will delve into compelling case studies that spotlight the successful integration of gamification in middle school classrooms. Middle school is a crucial phase in a student's educational journey, characterized by unique challenges and opportunities. These case studies showcase how gamified learning experiences have been designed to address the specific needs of middle school students, making education both engaging and impactful.

One outstanding example comes from a seventh-grade science class where the teacher introduced a gamified approach to teach complex scientific concepts. The class embarked on a virtual space exploration mission, with students becoming "space scientists." They were tasked with solving real-life scientific problems, such as analyzing data from Mars rovers or designing experiments for the International Space Station. Through this gamified scenario, students not only learned science but also developed critical thinking and problem-solving skills while collaborating with their peers.

Another inspiring case study comes from an eighth-grade history class. The teacher transformed the study of historical events into an immersive adventure. Students took on the roles of historical detectives and were presented with historical mysteries to solve. They analyzed primary sources, examined evidence, and even conducted mock trials to understand pivotal historical events. This gamified approach not only made history come alive but also fostered a deeper appreciation for the past and the importance of critical analysis.

In yet another instance, a sixth-grade mathematics teacher gamified the learning of algebraic concepts. Students became "math wizards" on a quest to rescue a magical kingdom from an enchantment. To progress in their quest, they had to solve algebraic equations and unlock the secrets of mathematics. This approach not only demystified algebra but also encouraged students to view math as a tool for solving real-world problems.

These middle school case studies demonstrate the potential of gamification in addressing the unique characteristics of middle school education. By incorporating elements of adventure, problem-solving, and role-playing, educators can make learning in middle school both enjoyable and academically enriching. Gamified experiences not only enhance subject knowledge but also cultivate crucial skills like teamwork, critical thinking, and a deeper appreciation for the subjects being taught. Middle school educators can draw inspiration from these examples to create engaging and effective learning environments for their students.

* * *

High School Implementations

Now, we'll delve into high school classrooms where gamification has been thoughtfully integrated to enhance the educational experience for students. High school education poses unique challenges, from motivating teenagers to preparing them for future endeavors. These case studies illustrate how gamified learning experiences have successfully addressed these challenges, fostering engagement, critical thinking, and preparation for higher education and careers.

One compelling example comes from a tenth-grade biology class where a teacher used gamification to teach complex biological concepts. The class embarked on a "biological expedition," with students taking on the roles of scientists exploring a fictional ecosystem. They collected data, conducted experiments, and even simulated ecological crises. This gamified approach not only deepened their understanding of biology but also honed their problem-solving skills and environmental awareness.

In another case, a high school history teacher introduced a gamified approach to studying world history. Students became "time travelers" and embarked on a journey through different historical periods. They had to solve historical mysteries, decode ancient texts, and make decisions that impacted the course of history. This approach not only made history engaging but also encouraged students to think critically about the consequences of historical events and decisions.

Furthermore, in a twelfth-grade economics class, the teacher incorporated gamification to teach financial literacy. Students became "financial wizards" on a quest to achieve financial independence. They managed virtual budgets, invested in simulated stock markets, and made decisions about saving and spending. This gamified approach not only equipped students with practical financial skills but also instilled a sense of responsibility and financial awareness.

These high school case studies exemplify the power of gamification in addressing the unique needs of high school education. By infusing elements of exploration, problem-solving, and decision-making into the curriculum, educators can prepare high school students not only for academic success but also for the challenges of adulthood. Gamified learning experiences foster critical thinking, responsibility, and a deeper understanding of the subjects being taught, making them valuable tools for high school educators to consider when designing their own curricula.

* * *

Lessons Learned and Best Practices

Let's dive into the valuable lessons learned from the gamification case studies discussed earlier and extract best practices that K-12 educators can apply when implementing gamified learning experiences in their classrooms. By examining these lessons and practices, educators can gain insights into how to make gamification a successful and enriching part of their teaching approach.

One crucial lesson is the importance of aligning gamified activities with educational goals. Gamification should not be a mere addition to the curriculum but a tool that enhances the achievement of specific learning objectives. Educators should clearly define the learning outcomes they aim to achieve through gamification and design activities that directly contribute to these goals.

Another valuable lesson is the need for ongoing assessment and feedback. Educators should continuously monitor the progress of their students within gamified experiences and provide timely feedback. This feedback loop not only helps students understand their strengths and areas for improvement but also allows educators to adapt and refine their gamified approaches for maximum effectiveness.

Additionally, the case studies emphasize the significance of student engagement. Gamification should be designed to capture students' interest and motivate them to participate actively. Incorporating elements of choice, competition, and exploration can be effective strategies for fostering engagement.

Moreover, educators should consider the diverse learning styles of their students. Gamified experiences can be tailored to accommodate various learning preferences, ensuring that all students have the opportunity to thrive in the gamified classroom.

Best practices for successful gamification include integrating game mechanics that align with the subject matter, creating immersive narratives that immerse students in the learning process, and ensuring a balance between challenge and skill level to prevent frustration or boredom.

Overall, the lessons learned and best practices I've highlighted provide a solid foundation for K-12 educators to embark on their gamification journey. By carefully planning, continuously assessing, and tailoring gamified experiences to their students' needs, educators can create engaging and effective learning environments that inspire curiosity and foster academic growth.

Global Perspectives on Educational Gamification

Let's take a look at the global impact of gamification in education, shedding light on how educators from different countries and regions have embraced this innovative approach. These diverse perspectives reveal the universality of the benefits of gamification while also highlighting unique cultural nuances and approaches to implementing gamified learning experiences.

One compelling aspect of global perspectives on educational gamification is the recognition of its ability to transcend cultural barriers. Gamification has proven to be effective in various educational settings worldwide, from densely populated urban areas to remote rural communities. It has become a versatile tool for educators to engage students regardless of their cultural backgrounds.

In Japan, for instance, educators have integrated gamification into the study of traditional arts such as calligraphy and tea ceremonies. By adding elements of competition and rewards to these cultural practices, students not only preserve their heritage but also find new enthusiasm for learning.

Similarly, in Kenya, gamified approaches have been employed to teach agricultural skills to students in rural communities. By transforming farming and agricultural practices into interactive games, students acquire valuable skills that are directly applicable to their daily lives.

Moreover, European countries have embraced gamification to enhance language learning. Students across Europe engage in language quests, where they earn points and rewards for successfully using new vocabulary and phrases. This approach has significantly boosted language acquisition and intercultural communication skills.

These global perspectives on educational gamification highlight the adaptability and effectiveness of this approach across different cultures and educational contexts. While the specific applications may vary, the underlying principles of engaging students through play, competition, and exploration remain consistent. K-12 educators can draw inspiration from these global examples to enrich their own gamified learning experiences and promote cross-cultural understanding among their students.

7

Overcoming Challenges and Obstacles

In the journey of integrating gamification into educational settings, it's inevitable to encounter a spectrum of challenges and obstacles. This chapter delves into these hurdles, offering practical strategies and insights to navigate them effectively.

Common Pitfalls and How to Avoid Them

When we start using games in our classrooms to make learning more fun, it's like stepping into a new adventure. We're excited, but sometimes we might stumble a bit. That's okay! Let's talk about some common mistakes and how we can dodge them, making our gamified learning journey smoother.

Starting Too Big, Too Fast: It's like jumping into the deep end of a pool before learning to swim. We might think we need fancy digital games right away, but that can be too much at first. Instead, let's start simple. Maybe we can turn a quiz into a fun game or use a simple point system for class participation. Then, as we get more comfortable, we can add cooler stuff.

Forgetting Why We're Playing: Remember, the main goal is to help our students learn better, not just to play games. Sometimes, we might get carried away with the game part and forget about the learning. To avoid this, let's always ask ourselves: "Is this game helping my students learn what they need to?" If the answer is "No," it's time to tweak the game.

Making It Too Hard or Too Easy: If our game is too hard, students might get frustrated. If it's too easy, they might get bored. We need to find that sweet spot where the game is just right. This means picking games that match what our students already know and what they need to learn next.

Not Listening to Our Students: Our students are the ones playing these games, so their thoughts are super important. If they find something too tricky or not fun, they'll tell us. We just need to make sure we're listening and ready to make changes based on what they say.

Sticking to Just One Way: There isn't just one way to add games to learning. What works in one class might not work in another. So, if something isn't going well, it's okay to try something different. Keep exploring and experimenting with different games and activities.

By knowing these common mistakes, we can be better prepared to make learning fun and effective through games. Remember, it's all about helping our students learn in a way that's enjoyable and exciting for them. Let's take it one step at a time and watch our classrooms transform into amazing learning adventures!

Managing Classroom Dynamics

When we bring games into our classrooms, it's like adding a splash of color to a painting – it can make learning come alive! But just like artists, we need to make sure all the colors blend well. This means managing how our students interact with each other and the game, so everyone has a good time and learns a lot.

Understanding Each Student: Our classrooms are like gardens with different kinds of flowers – each student is unique. Some might love competition, while others might prefer working together. Some might catch on to games quickly, others might need a bit more time. It's important for us to know these differences. This way, we can pick games that everyone can enjoy and learn from.

Creating Roles and Teams: Imagine a game where everyone wants to be the captain – it would be chaotic, right? In our gamified classrooms, we can assign different roles to students based on what they're good at and what they like. Maybe one student is great at keeping score, while another is good at explaining rules. By creating roles and teams, we make sure everyone has a special part to play. This helps students feel important and work better together.

Keeping Things Fair and Fun: Games should always be fun and fair. If a game is too hard or too easy, or if some students always win, it's not much fun for everyone else. We need to keep an eye on how games are going and make little changes if needed to keep things balanced. Maybe we can change the rules a bit, or mix up the teams. The goal is to make sure every student feels like they have a chance to succeed and enjoy the game.

Building a Positive Game Culture: Just like we have rules for behavior in class, we need rules for our games too. Rules like taking turns, being kind to each other, and being a good sport whether we win or lose. These rules help create a happy and respectful environment where everyone feels safe to participate and learn.

Encouraging Everyone to Participate: Sometimes, some students might be shy or think they're not good at games. We need to encourage them and show them that their ideas and efforts are valuable. Maybe we can give them roles that don't require them to be in the spotlight but still let them be part of the action.

By understanding and managing the way our students interact in gamified learning, we create a classroom that's not just about learning – it's about having a great time together while learning. It's like being the conductor of an orchestra, making sure every instrument plays its part to create beautiful music!

Dealing with Resistance to Change

Introducing games into learning is a bit like planting a new type of flower in your garden. Not everyone might like it at first. Some students and even fellow teachers might be hesitant about this new way of learning. They might prefer the usual ways because it's what they know and feel comfortable with. But don't worry, there are ways to help everyone get on board with this exciting change!

Talking About the 'Why': Imagine you're about to go on a trip. Wouldn't you want to know where you're going and why? It's the same with gamification. Start by explaining why you're using games in class. Tell your students and colleagues how these games can make learning more fun and help everyone understand things better. Share stories or examples of how games have helped other classes. When people understand the 'why,' they are more likely to give it a try.

Showing, Not Just Telling: Sometimes, seeing is believing. You could show a short video of a class where games are being used for learning. Or maybe after trying a small game in class, discuss with your students what they learned and how they felt. When people see the benefits with their own eyes, they might feel more excited about the change.

Starting Small: Change can be scary, so it's okay to start slow. You don't have to turn every lesson into a game overnight. Maybe start with a short, simple game once a week. As everyone starts to enjoy it and see how it helps, you can slowly add more games.

Listening and Adapting: Remember, it's okay if not everyone loves the idea at first. Listen to what they are worried about. Maybe they're afraid they won't do well in the games, or they think it might be too distracting. By listening, you can understand their concerns and make changes. Maybe you can adjust the game to make it feel more comfortable for them.

Celebrating Small Wins: When your class completes a game and learns something new, celebrate it! Maybe have a little cheer or a special sticker for everyone. Celebrating makes everyone feel good and shows that this change is something positive.

Dealing with resistance to change is all about understanding, patience, and small steps. It's like nurturing a plant. With a bit of care and time, it will grow and become something beautiful. And soon, your classroom will be a fun and exciting place where everyone loves to learn!

Balancing Gaming and Learning

When we mix games with learning, it's like making a new recipe in the kitchen. We need to get the balance just right – too much sugar and it's too sweet, not enough flour and it doesn't hold together. In our classrooms, we have to find the perfect mix between the fun of gaming and the serious business of learning.

Keeping Our Eyes on the Prize: Learning is always the main dish, and games are the seasoning that makes it tastier. We need to remember that the games we choose should help our students learn what we're trying to teach. For example, if we're teaching multiplication, we might use a game where students earn points for solving math problems. This way, they're having fun and learning at the same time.

Games as Tools, Not Distractions: Think of games as a toolbox. Each game is a tool that can help fix a specific learning challenge. We don't want our students to just play games for the sake of playing. Instead, each game should have a clear purpose, like helping students understand a tough concept or remember something important.

Adjusting as We Go: Not every game works out perfectly the first time. Maybe a game is too hard, or maybe it's not as fun as we thought. That's okay! We can tweak the rules, or change the game a bit to make it better. It's like adjusting a recipe until it tastes just right.

Checking In with Our Students: Our students are the taste-testers of our recipe. We need to ask them how they feel about the games. Do they find them fun? Are they learning from them? Their feedback is super important to help us find that perfect balance.

Not All Games for All Times: Just like we don't eat dessert for every meal, we don't need to use games in every lesson. Sometimes the traditional way of teaching is the best way. It's all about using games when they add something special to the learning experience.

Finding the right balance between gaming and learning is all about experimenting, adjusting, and listening. It's a fun and creative process that can make our classes more exciting and effective. When we get it right, our students learn more, and they have a great time doing it. It's like creating a favorite recipe that everyone loves!

Continual Improvement and Adaptation

Think of using games in our classrooms like growing a garden. Just planting seeds isn't enough; we need to water them, maybe move them into the sun, or even change the soil sometimes. This is what continual improvement and adaptation in gamified learning is all about – it's never just 'set it and forget it'.

Watching and Learning: As we use games in our lessons, it's important to keep our eyes open. How are the students responding? Are they getting more excited about learning? Are they understanding the lessons better? Just like a gardener watches their plants, we need to watch how our games are affecting our students and our teaching.

Gathering Feedback: Feedback is like the sunshine and water for our garden. We should regularly ask our students what they think about the games. Which ones do they like? Which ones don't work so well for them? Their thoughts and feelings can help us make better choices about the games we use.

Being Ready to Change: Sometimes, a game that we thought would be great might not work as we expected. Or maybe our students have outgrown a game. When this happens, it's okay to change things. We can try a different game or modify the one we're using. It's all about being flexible and ready to make changes for the better.

Staying Curious and Learning More: The world of gamified learning is always growing and changing. There are always new games and new ideas. As teachers, we should stay curious and keep learning. We can read about new games, talk to other teachers, or attend workshops. This helps us bring fresh and exciting ideas to our classrooms.

Reflecting on Our Practices: Just like a gardener sits back and thinks about what's working and what's not, we should regularly reflect on our teaching practices. Are the games helping our students learn better? Are we using them in the best way? Reflection helps us understand what we're doing well and what we can do better.

Continual improvement and adaptation in gamified learning is all about being attentive, open to feedback, flexible, curious, and reflective. It's a journey of growth and learning, not just for our students, but for us as educators. Just like a well-tended garden, our classrooms can become vibrant places of learning and joy.

8

Assessment and Feedback in Gamified Learning

Formative and Summative Assessments

When we bring the exciting world of gamification into our classrooms, it's important to think about how we check what our students have learned. There are two main types of assessments we use in education: formative and summative. Understanding these two and using them in gamified learning can really help us see how much our students are growing and learning.

Formative assessments are like little checkpoints along the way in the learning journey. They're not about giving grades but about seeing where students are and what they need next. Imagine you're playing a video game, and at certain points, you get small challenges to test your skills. These challenges help you understand what you've learned and what you need to practice more. That's what formative assessments do in the classroom. They can be quick quizzes, class discussions, or even a project that's part of the game you're using in class. The great thing about formative assessments in gamified learning is that they can be a natural and fun part of the game, making it easier for students to show what they know without the pressure of a big test.

Summative assessments, on the other hand, are like the big boss battle at the end of a video game. They come after a period of learning and give students a chance to show everything they've learned. In the classroom, these can be final projects, big tests, or presentations. When using gamification, summative assessments can be part of a larger, more complex challenge in the game. They help teachers see how well the students have understood the whole unit or course. It's important to make these assessments fair and clear, so students know what's expected of them.

Both formative and summative assessments are important in gamified learning. Formative assessments help us guide our students' learning journey day by day, while summative assessments let us see the big picture of what they've learned. Together, they help us make sure that our fun, game-based learning is also effective and that our students are really getting the most out of their educational adventures.

Integrating Assessment into Game Mechanics

In gamified learning, we can blend assessments seamlessly into the games themselves. This means that evaluating students' understanding becomes part of the fun and adventure of the game. Let's explore how we can make this happen in a way that's enjoyable and effective for students.

One way to integrate assessments into game mechanics is through levels and challenges within the game. As students progress through different levels, they encounter questions or problems related to what they're learning. Think of it like a video game where each level tests a different skill. When students answer correctly or solve a problem, they move on to the next level. This way, they're being assessed without the pressure of a traditional test.

Another method is to use in-game points or rewards. Students earn points for correct answers or for demonstrating understanding of a concept. These points can lead to rewards within the game, like unlocking a new character or a new part of the story. This not only motivates students but also helps teachers track how well each student understands the material.

We can also use characters or storylines in the game to ask questions directly related to the lesson. For example, in a history game, a character might ask the player to explain a historical event. The student's answer can show how well they've understood the topic. This method makes assessment a natural part of the game's story, keeping students engaged and learning.

Feedback is another important aspect. In gamified learning, feedback should be immediate and constructive. When a student makes a mistake, the game can offer hints or explanations to help them understand the correct answer. This kind of instant feedback is really helpful for learning and makes students feel supported as they play and learn.

Integrating assessment into game mechanics makes learning more dynamic and interactive. It helps students engage with the material in a deeper way and allows teachers to evaluate learning in a more natural, less stressful environment. This way, assessment becomes a fun and integral part of the learning journey, not something separate and daunting.

Student Feedback and Involvement

In gamified learning, it's not just about how we, as teachers, assess our students; it's also about listening to what our students have to say. Student feedback and involvement are key parts of making learning fun and effective. When students are involved in giving feedback, they feel more invested in their learning, and we get valuable insights into how we can make our teaching even better.

One way to involve students is by asking them to give feedback on the games and activities they do in class. After playing a learning game, we can have a discussion or ask students to write down what they liked about the game, what they found challenging, and what they think could be improved. This feedback can be really helpful for us to understand what works and what doesn't in our gamified lessons.

We can also encourage students to suggest ideas for games or gamified activities. Maybe they have an idea for a new game level or a fun way to earn points. By involving students in creating the games, we make the learning experience more meaningful to them. It's like they're helping to build their own learning adventure, which can be really exciting and motivating.

Another important part of student feedback is reflecting on their own learning. We can ask students to think about what they've learned from the game and how it has helped them understand the subject better. This reflection can be done through a class discussion, a writing activity, or even a digital journal entry. It helps students process what they've learned and gives them a chance to voice their own thoughts about their learning journey.

Finally, involving students in setting goals for their learning can be very effective. Before starting a gamified activity, we can discuss what each student hopes to achieve or learn from the game. Then, after the activity, we can revisit these goals and see how well they were met. This not only gives students a sense of control over their learning but also helps them stay focused and motivated.

Involving students in giving feedback and participating in their own learning process makes gamified learning more interactive and personal. It helps build a learning environment where students feel heard and valued, and where they're active participants in their own education. Gather and use student feedback; involve students in creating and reflecting on their gamified learning experiences.

Grading in a Gamified Classroom

Grading in a classroom where learning is like playing a game might sound tricky, but it can actually be a smooth and fair process. In a gamified classroom, we grade students not just on their answers to questions, but on how they play the game and what they learn from it.

In this kind of classroom, points or scores in the game can be part of how we grade. For example, students might earn points for completing challenges, helping classmates, or showing they understand a lesson. But it's not just about getting the highest score. It's also about how students approach problems and work through them. Even if they don't get the right answer at first, if they keep trying and learn from their mistakes, that's really important and can be part of their grade too.

We can also use badges or levels in the game to show how students are doing. For instance, earning a badge might mean a student has mastered a certain skill, like multiplication in math. Moving up a level might show that they understand a big part of the subject, like finishing a unit on ancient history. This way, grading becomes more about what students have learned and achieved, not just the numbers they get on a test.

Another important part of grading in a gamified classroom is feedback. This means telling students not just what grades they got, but why they got them. Feedback can be given in the game itself, like comments on how they solved a problem, or in person by the teacher. This feedback helps students understand what they're doing well and what they need to work on, which is a big part of learning.

Sometimes, we might even ask students to grade themselves or each other. They can think about how well they did in the game, what they learned, and give themselves a grade. Or, they can watch how their classmates play and learn, and give them helpful feedback. This not only makes grading fairer but also teaches students to think about their own learning and be kind and helpful to others.

Grading in a gamified classroom is about looking at the whole picture of a student's learning. It's not just about right or wrong answers, but about how students engage with the game, solve problems, and grow in their understanding of the subject. You will want to explore ways to make grading in gamified learning effective, fair, and meaningful for students, focusing on their overall development and learning journey.

Reflecting on Teaching Practices

Reflecting on teaching practices is like taking a step back and looking at the big picture of how we teach. In a gamified classroom, this means thinking about how well the games and activities are helping our students learn and grow. It's an important part of being a teacher because it helps us keep getting better at our job.

First, we think about the games and activities we've used. We ask ourselves questions like: Are the students really enjoying these games? Are they learning what they're supposed to from them? Sometimes a game might be fun, but it doesn't help much with learning. Other times, a game might be really educational, but the students don't find it very interesting. Finding the right balance is key.

We also look at how the games are affecting the classroom. Are the students working well together? Are they excited to come to class and play the games? We want our classroom to be a place where students are happy and eager to learn. If the games are making the classroom a better place for learning, that's a good sign.

Another important part of reflecting is listening to our students. We can learn a lot by just asking them what they think about the games and activities. They might have some great ideas for making the games even better or tell us about things we didn't realize weren't working so well.

We also think about our own teaching. Are we explaining the games clearly? Are we making sure every student understands and gets to participate? Sometimes, we might need to change the way we teach to make the games more effective.

Lastly, we think about what we can do better next time. Maybe we need to choose different games, change the way we play them, or find new ways to help our students learn. Reflecting on our teaching practices helps us keep improving and making learning fun and effective for every student.

9

Ethical Considerations and Future Directions

Ethical Aspects of Gamification

When we talk about bringing games into learning, it's really important to think about the ethical aspects, which means making sure that we're using gamification in a way that's fair and good for all students. Ethical considerations are like the rules that help us make sure everyone is treated right and feels safe and happy while learning.

One big part of this is making sure that the games are fair for everyone. This means that all students, no matter who they are or where they come from, should be able to play and learn from the games. The games shouldn't favor some students over others. For example, a game shouldn't be easier for students who are really good at reading if it's supposed to be teaching math. Everyone should have an equal chance to succeed and enjoy the game.

Another important thing to think about is privacy. When students use digital games, they might need to share some of their information, like their names or how they're doing in the game. It's important to make sure that this information is kept safe and private. This means only using it to help them learn better and not letting anyone else see it without a good reason.

We also need to be careful about how we use rewards and points in the games. If the games make students feel bad for not getting high scores or not earning as many rewards as others, that's not fair. We want to use points and rewards to make learning fun and motivate students, not to make them feel upset or like they're not as good as their classmates.

It's also important to think about how the games might affect students' feelings. We want to make sure that the games don't make any students feel left out or upset. For instance, a game should include characters and stories that are respectful and considerate of all kinds of people and cultures.

Finally, we should always ask ourselves if the games are really helping students learn. The main goal of using games in education is to make learning better and more fun. If a game isn't doing that, then we need to think about how we can change it or find a different one that works better.

The Future of Gamification in Education

Thinking about the future of gamification in education is like looking into a crystal ball to see how learning could become even more exciting and helpful for students. As technology keeps getting better, the way we use games in the classroom will change and grow too.

One big change we might see is more virtual reality (VR) and augmented reality (AR) in schools. VR and AR can take students on amazing learning adventures, like walking through ancient cities or diving deep into the ocean, all without leaving the classroom. This means students can experience and learn about things that are hard to see or understand in real life.

Another exciting thing in the future could be games that are more personalized for each student. Just like how some video games change based on who's playing, educational games could adapt to each student's learning style and pace. This means the game could become more challenging if a student is doing really well, or it could offer extra help if a student is having a hard time.

We might also see more games that help with social and emotional learning. These games could teach students important skills like how to work well with others, how to solve problems peacefully, or how to be a good friend. Learning these skills is just as important as learning subjects like math or science.

Another important part of the future of gamification is making sure that everyone has access to these games and technologies. This means schools everywhere, no matter if they're in big cities or small towns, should be able to use these tools to help their students learn.

Finally, we'll probably see more research on how gamification helps with learning. This research will help teachers understand the best ways to use games in education and will show us new ideas for making learning even better with gamification.

The future of gamification in education is full of opportunities to make learning more fun, effective, and accessible for everyone.

Preparing for Technological Advancements

As we look towards the future of education, it's like getting ready for a big adventure. We know that new technologies are coming, and they're going to change how we teach and learn. Preparing for these changes means we can make the most of them and help all our students learn better.

One important step in getting ready is to keep learning about new technologies. This means teachers might need to take classes or workshops to learn about the latest gadgets and software. Just like students learn new things in school, teachers need to keep learning too, especially about technology.

Another key part of preparing is making sure our schools have the right equipment. This could mean having enough computers or tablets for students, or maybe even special gear for virtual reality lessons. It's like making sure you have all the right tools before you start a big project.

We also need to think about how to use these technologies in the best way. This means figuring out how they can fit into our lessons and help with the subjects we're teaching. It's not just about having cool gadgets; it's about using them to make learning more interesting and helpful.

It's also important to make sure everyone is included. This means making sure that all students, no matter where they live or how much money their families have, get to use these new technologies. We want everyone to have the same chance to learn with these exciting tools.

Finally, preparing for new technology means being ready to change how we do things. This can be hard sometimes, but it's important to be flexible and open to new ideas. Technology changes fast, and what works today might be different tomorrow. We need to be ready to try new things and find the best ways to help our students learn.

Preparing for technological advancements is a big part of making sure that we can give our students the best education possible, now and in the future.

Fostering Lifelong Learning through Gamification

When we use games in learning, we're not just teaching students about math, science, or history. We're also helping them love learning and want to keep learning for their whole lives. This is what we call fostering lifelong learning, and it's like planting a seed that grows into a love for discovering new things.

One way gamification helps with lifelong learning is by making education fun and exciting. When students play educational games, they often don't even realize they're learning because they're having so much fun. It's like when you're playing your favorite game and you don't want to stop. This excitement can make students want to keep learning more, even outside of school.

Gamification also teaches students important skills like problem-solving, critical thinking, and creativity. In games, students often have to think of new ways to solve problems or make decisions that affect the outcome of the game. These skills are not just important for school; they're skills that will help students in all parts of their lives, now and in the future.

Another great thing about gamification is that it helps students feel confident. When they succeed in a game, they feel proud and believe in themselves more. This confidence can encourage them to take on new challenges, not just in school, but in all areas of life.

Games also show students that it's okay to make mistakes. In many games, you have to try different things and sometimes fail before you find the right way to win. This teaches students that making mistakes is part of learning and helps them not be afraid to try new things.

Finally, gamification can connect learning to the real world. Some games are about real-life problems, like protecting the environment or helping a community. Playing these games can make students more interested in these topics and want to learn more about them, even after they leave the classroom.

Fostering lifelong learning through gamification is about helping students love learning and stay curious, always.

Staying Informed and Adaptable

Things are always changing, especially when it comes to using games for learning. Staying informed and adaptable means keeping up with these changes and being ready to try new things in our classrooms. It's like being a detective who is always looking for clues about the best ways to teach and help students learn.

Staying informed means we, as teachers, need to keep learning. This can be done by reading books and articles about new teaching methods and technologies, going to teacher training workshops, and talking with other teachers about what they're doing in their classrooms. It's like collecting pieces of a puzzle that, when put together, can help us teach better.

Being adaptable means being ready to change the way we teach when we find new methods or tools that can help our students. Sometimes, a way of teaching that worked really well last year might not be the best this year. Or, we might find a new game or app that can help our students learn in a way we didn't think of before. Being adaptable is like being a chef who is always trying new recipes to see what tastes best.

It's also important to listen to our students and get their ideas and feedback. They can tell us what they like about the games we're using and what they think could be better. This helps us stay informed about what's working and what's not, and it makes our students feel like they're a part of their own learning.

Finally, staying informed and adaptable helps us prepare for the future. The world is changing fast, and the jobs our students will have when they grow up might be very different from the jobs people have today. By keeping up with new teaching methods and technologies, we can help our students be ready for whatever the future holds.

Staying informed and adaptable is all about being the best teachers we can be, for our students today and for their futures.

10

Creating a Gamified Classroom Culture

Building a Supportive Learning Environment

Creating a supportive learning environment is like building a safe and happy home for learning in your classroom. This means making a place where every student feels welcome, valued, and ready to learn. When we use gamification, it's important to create an environment where students feel comfortable taking risks and trying new things without fear of making mistakes.

One key to building this kind of environment is making sure everyone feels included. This means creating games and activities that are fun and interesting for all students, no matter who they are or where they come from. It's like making sure every player in a game has a chance to play and succeed.

Another important part is encouraging teamwork and friendship among students. When students work together in games, they learn to help each other and solve problems together. It's like being part of a team where everyone has a role to play and everyone's contributions are important.

We also need to make sure that our classroom is a place where mistakes are okay. In games, it's normal to try something and fail a few times before you succeed. We want our students to feel that it's okay to make mistakes in the classroom too. This helps them be brave enough to try new things and learn from their mistakes.

Respect is another big part of a supportive learning environment. This means students and teachers treat each other kindly and listen to each other's ideas. It's like playing a game where everyone follows the rules and respects the other players.

Finally, keeping the classroom fun and exciting is important. This means changing games and activities often so students are always interested and looking forward to what comes next. It's like adding new levels to a game to keep it challenging and fun.

Building a supportive learning environment is the first step in creating a classroom where gamification helps every student learn and grow.

Engaging with Parents and the Community

Engaging with parents and the community is like opening the doors of your classroom to the world outside. It's about sharing what's happening in your gamified classroom and getting everyone involved in the learning process. This helps everyone understand how games are helping students learn and grow.

First, it's important to communicate with parents. This means telling them about the games and activities you're using in the classroom and how they help with learning. You can do this through newsletters, emails, or even special events like a 'Game Night' at school where parents can come and play the educational games with their students. It's like giving parents a peek into the classroom so they can see the fun and learning happening.

You can also involve the community in your gamified classroom. This could be inviting local businesses or experts to participate in the games or to share their knowledge. For example, if you're playing a game about building a city, you could invite an architect or city planner to talk about their job. This helps students see how what they're learning connects to the real world.

Another way to engage with parents and the community is by getting their feedback and ideas. Parents might have great suggestions for games or activities based on what their children enjoy at home. Community members could offer resources or expertise that can make the games even more exciting and educational.

It's also important to show parents and the community the positive effects of gamification. This might mean sharing students' progress and achievements, like a project they completed as part of a game. This helps everyone see how gamification is making a difference in students' learning.

Finally, engaging with parents and the community can also mean involving them in the challenges or goals of the games. For instance, if students are playing a game about helping the environment, you could organize a community clean-up day where students, parents, and community members work together.

Engaging with parents and the community helps build a strong support system for students and makes learning a shared journey for everyone.

Continuous Professional Development

Continuous professional development for teachers is like always being a student ourselves. It means we keep learning new things, especially about how to make our classrooms more fun and effective with gamification. Just like our students are always learning, we as teachers need to keep growing and getting better too.

One way to keep developing professionally is by going to teacher workshops and training sessions. These are special classes where teachers can learn about new games and technologies and how to use them in the classroom. It's like going back to school to learn new tricks and skills that we can bring back to our students.

Another way to keep growing as a teacher is by reading books and articles about gamification and education. There are lots of experts out there who write about the best ways to use games in teaching. By reading their ideas, we can learn a lot of new strategies and tips for making our classrooms even better.

We can also learn a lot by talking with other teachers. This could be teachers in our own school or teachers from all over the world. Nowadays, we can connect with other educators online through websites and social media groups.

It's like having a big team of teachers to share ideas with and get advice from.

Trying out new things in our classroom is also a big part of professional development. This means not being afraid to try a new game or change the way we teach a lesson. Sometimes, we might try something that doesn't work, but that's okay. Every time we try, we learn something that can help us be better teachers.

Finally, it's important to reflect on our own teaching. After trying a new game or teaching method, we can think about what went well and what could be better next time. This reflection helps us understand our teaching more and keeps us moving forward.

Continuous professional development is all about staying curious and excited about teaching, just like we want our students to be about learning.

Sustaining Interest and Engagement Over Time

Keeping students interested and engaged over time in a gamified classroom is like keeping a fire burning. Just like a fire needs more wood to keep it going, we need to keep adding new and exciting things to our classroom games to keep students' interest alive.

One way to do this is by updating our games and activities regularly. This means adding new challenges, levels, or even new games to our lessons. It's like when you get a new level in a video game – it makes the game more exciting and keeps you wanting to play.

Another way to keep students engaged is by involving them in the creation of the games. When students help make the games or come up with ideas for them, they're more likely to be interested in playing. It's like they're the chefs helping to cook a meal; they're going to want to eat it because they helped make it.

We can also keep interest high by connecting the games to real-world problems or situations. If students see how the games relate to things happening in the world or in their own lives, they're more likely to care about the game. For example, a game about building a city can teach them about community planning and the environment, which are real things they see every day.

Celebrating achievements is also important. When students reach a goal in a game or do well, celebrating these achievements can make them feel proud and want to keep trying. This could be as simple as giving out certificates or having a special mention in class.

Lastly, it's important to keep the games fair and balanced. This means making sure the games aren't too easy or too hard and that every student has a chance to succeed. If a game is too easy, students might get bored, and if it's too hard, they might get frustrated. Finding the right balance keeps everyone happy and interested.

Keeping students interested and engaged is like keeping that fire burning – it takes work and attention, but it's what makes learning exciting and fun.

11

Conclusion

Final Thoughts and Encouragement for Educators

As we come to the end of our journey together, it's like reaching the final level of a long, exciting game. We've explored lots of ideas and strategies, but the adventure doesn't stop here. Remember, as educators, we're always learning and growing, just like our students.

First, it's important to remember that gamification is a tool, not a magic solution. It's a way to make learning more fun and engaging, but it works best when combined with other teaching methods. Think of it like adding a special ingredient to a recipe – it can make the dish better, but you still need all the other ingredients.

Also, don't be afraid to try new things and make mistakes. Trying a new game or activity in your classroom can be a bit scary, but it's also exciting. Sometimes things won't go as planned, and that's okay. Every mistake is a chance to learn and get better.

It's also important to keep your students at the center of everything you do. Every game or activity should be about helping them learn and grow. Listen to their feedback, watch how they play and learn, and keep adjusting your games to meet their needs.

Remember to be patient. Building a gamified classroom culture doesn't happen overnight. It takes time to find the right games, learn how to use them, and see how they fit into your teaching. Just like in a game, there are levels to pass and challenges to overcome.

Finally, know that what you're doing is important. By using gamification, you're not just teaching subjects; you're helping students develop a love for learning. You're giving them skills like problem-solving, teamwork, and creativity that they'll use for the rest of their lives.

Lastly, I want to say thank you for your hard work and dedication. Being an educator is one of the most important jobs in the world. I know that sounds cliche, but it's truly how I feel. Keep learning, keep trying new things, and keep making a difference in your students' lives. Your journey as a gamified educator is an adventure that can make learning an unforgettable experience for you and your students.

* * *

Thank You

As I close this chapter on creating a gamified classroom culture, I hope that you've found valuable insights and inspiration to bring a new level of engagement and excitement to your teaching. Remember, your journey in gamification is as unique and dynamic as the elements you introduce in your classroom.

I would love to hear about your experiences and thoughts about this book. Your feedback is incredibly important to me, as it helps me understand what resonates with you, what challenges you face, and how I can improve this resource. Please take a moment to leave a review, sharing your thoughts and experiences. Your input not only supports me but also aids fellow educators in their journey towards creating more interactive and engaging learning environments. Thank you for being a part of this adventure, and I look forward to reading your valuable insights!

About the Author

John Riggs is a veteran educator with over 10 years of experience making learning fun and engaging for his students. After receiving his B.S. in Elementary Education from Fort Hays State University, John began his teaching career in elementary classrooms before transitioning to teaching middle school math and literature.

In 2016, John stumbled upon the concept of gamification and saw the potential to captivate students by making learning more game-like. He began experimenting with gamification techniques in his own classrooms and witnessed significantly increased student motivation, engagement, and academic performance.

Since then, John has become a firm believer in leveraging gamification to create dynamic, interactive learning experiences for students. He founded Education Unboxed, a platform dedicated to providing educators with gamification resources and training.

John lives in the Kansas City suburbs with his wife Michelle, two daughters, and their dogs. When he's not teaching John enjoys volunteering, reading sci-fi novels, and rooting for the Kansas City Chiefs and the Kansas City Royals.

You can connect with me on:

🌐 https://www.jriggs.net

f https://www.facebook.com/journey.wanderer

Subscribe to my newsletter:

✉ https://onlyawanderer.medium.com

Also by John Riggs

Author John Riggs draws from his 10+ years of experience revamping his own elementary and middle school classes with gamification. His work guides you step-by-step through concepts like rewards, competition, storytelling, and technology integration to create interactive, game-inspired learning environments.

Game On! Level Up Your Teaching With Gamification Transform your classroom and captivate your students with gamified learning! This practical book equips educators with strategies and tools to integrate game elements into their teaching. Learn how to boost student engagement, motivation, and academic achievement.